—MASTERING THE ART OF—
COMMUNICATION

Harness the Transformative Power of Active Listening, Craft Compelling Messages, Transform Conflict Into Collaboration, and Win Your Day

by

J P PATHAK

Email: jppathak1@gmail.com

Copyright © 2024 by J P Pathak

All rights reserved. No part of this book may be reproduced in any form without permission in writing from the author.

No part of this publication may be reproduced or transmitted in any form or by any means, mechanical or electronic, including photocopying or recording, by any information storage and retrieval system, or by email or any other means whatsoever without permission in writing from the author.

DEDICATION

To My *Dear Mother*,

"Your unwavering love, wisdom, and remarkable ability to listen deeply have left an indelible mark on my life and this book. Your guidance and encouragement, especially in our profession and social impact discussions, have shaped my understanding of communication and its profound significance. Though you are no longer with us, your presence is felt every moment. Your spirit lives on these pages, and so do the hearts of all those who cherish your memory. With deepest love and gratitude, this book is dedicated to you."

With Love and Gratitude.

J P Pathak

ACKNOWLEDGMENT

I want to express my sincere gratitude to everyone who contributed to the creation of this book.

I want to thank my family and friends for their unwavering support and encouragement throughout this journey. Your belief in me has been a constant source of inspiration.

I am deeply grateful to my best friend, Subodh, for his unwavering support and friendship throughout the journey of writing this book. Subodh's insightful feedback, constructive criticism, and encouragement have been invaluable in shaping the ideas and refining the content of this book. His keen intellect and thoughtful perspective have challenged me to strive for excellence in every aspect of this project.

Beyond his contribution to this book, Subodh has been a pillar of strength and inspiration in my life. His friendship has enriched my experience and brought joy to my days; I am genuinely grateful. Your collaboration and expertise have been instrumental in shaping this book into its final form.

Thank you, Subodh, for your friendship, wisdom, and unwavering belief in me and my work. Your presence in my life is a constant source of encouragement and support, and I am honored to have you as a friend.

Finally, I would like to thank the readers for their interest in this book. The insights and acknowledgments shared within these pages will prove valuable and enriching to all who engage with them.

J P Pathak

WHY IS THIS BOOK FOR YOU?

Unlock the secrets of effective communication and transform your relationships with **'Mastering the Art of Communication.'**

This insightful guide is your comprehensive roadmap to:

- Enhancing interpersonal skills
- Cultivating meaningful connections, and
- Conquering communication challenges with confidence and clarity

Through assertiveness training, conflict resolution techniques, and practical strategies, this book equips you with the tools to communicate with:

- Precision
- Empathy, and
- Authenticity in any situation

Drawing on timeless wisdom, real-life examples, and interactive exercises, you'll learn to become a more attentive listener, express yourself clearly, and build rapport effortlessly.

Whether you're navigating workplace dynamics, managing conflicts in personal relationships, or honing your public speaking skills, '**Mastering the Art of Communication**' provides invaluable insights and actionable advice to achieve your communication goals.

Focusing on fostering empathy, understanding, and respect, this book empowers readers to create deeper connections and unlock new opportunities for personal and professional growth.

Whether you're a seasoned communicator or just starting, this guide offers timeless wisdom and practical guidance for navigating the complexities of human interaction with confidence, clarity, and compassion.

Don't settle for mediocre connections—embrace the power of communication and unlock a world of possibilities with '**Mastering the Art of Communication.**'

Your journey to meaningful connections starts now!

TABLE OF CONTENTS

INTRODUCTION 11

PRINCIPLES OF EFFECTIVE COMMUNICATION 19

ACTIVE LISTENING 29

    EXERCISE 31

ROLE OF ACTIVE LISTENING IN COMMUNICATION 33

EMPATHY 37

    EXERCISE 44

PERSUASION 47

    WHAT IS PERSUASION? 47

    STORYTIME 48

FOSTERING MEANINGFUL CONNECTIONS 55

    STORYTIME 55

    BENEFITS 59

    COLLEGE LIFE 61

    PERSONAL LIFE 61

    PROFESSIONAL LIFE 62

    SOCIAL LIFE 62

    LONG-TERM SUCCESS 63

    STORYTIME 63

COMMUNICATION BARRIERS 69

    EXERCISE 72

    QUESTIONS 72

MY MESSAGE TO BUILDING RAPPORT ... 72
THE POWER OF ASSERTIVE COMMUNICATION ... 75
PASSIVE COMMUNICATION ... 75
ASSERTIVE COMMUNICATION ... 76
STORYTIME ... 76
LESSONS LEARNED ... 77
PRINCIPLES OF ASSERTIVE COMMUNICATION ... 78
EXERCISE ... 84
CALL FOR ACTION ... 85
SUMMARY AND TAKE-HOME MESSAGE ... 87
CHAPTER 1 ... 87
CHAPTER 2 ... 88
CHAPTER 3 ... 90
CHAPTER 4 ... 91
CHAPTER 5 ... 91
CHAPTER 6 ... 92
FINAL CHAPTER- CALL FOR ACTION ... 93
FINAL STORY ... 94
ABOUT THE AUTHOR ... 97
OTHER BOOKS WRITTEN BY THE AUTHOR ... 99
DISCLAIMER ... 101
MAY I ASK YOU A FAVOR? ... 103

INTRODUCTION

"Nothing in life is more important than communicating effectively."

- Gerald R. Ford

I have always been curious about effective communication, especially when thinking about my childhood in the village. Ramdas remains our guide and central character as we continue our journey towards success. This is our fifth milestone, and in the previous four episodes, we have discovered the one thing that makes a big difference in the life of a leader. In our first episode, "The One Thing That Will Make You an Effective Leader," we learned about the key traits distinguishing influential leaders. The second episode, "How to Go Beyond Strength," explored becoming a strong and effective leader. Episode three, "Rising Together," shifted the focus to teamwork and collaboration, exploring the importance of trust, communication, and shared vision in achieving shared goals. In episode four, "Mastering the Art of Goal Setting," Ramdas shared invaluable lessons on navigating the journey towards success, including setting and achieving meaningful goals.

Let me remind you about the fear of dacoits among the villagers of my community and how Ramdas created web-coded communication that helped them overcome the fear. He also became a hero to all.

Once we overcame the fear and celebrated the success of teamwork, I asked my father about my question. What is Effective Communication? My father looked at Ramdas and encouraged him to share his experience and how he could manage that difficult situation smoothly.

Ramdas started sharing his success story with us. Let us learn from his experience.

We struggled to communicate among ourselves (mobile phones were not there, and the village needed electricity), but we knew what communication was. My job was to make it effective.

So, as per Ramdas, effective communication means passing on the message or thoughts to another group and from that group to the next group. The challenge was to keep the message intact with no distortion. So, it is essential to select a method or channel very carefully so that the message is understood by a group clearly. Success is in delivering the message to my satisfaction.

As a small boy, I raised my doubt to Ramdas. How do you know your message was delivered to the last group, and is the exact message you initiated? With a smile, he looked at his Guru Ji, appreciated my point first, and gave me complete clarity. I am happy to share my learning.

Effective communication: Communication can be defined as the act of passing on or sharing ideas, opinions, knowledge, or information. A leader must carefully choose the method or channel of communication to ensure that the intended purpose is achieved. Good leaders always check for their team's understanding and encourage feedback to ensure effective communication.

During those days in my village when Ramdas led the primary team and coordinated with four subgroups, I learned that a leader could communicate in various ways.

For example:

1. **Verbal Communication:** Ramdas held regular meetings where he spoke directly to the villagers. He was trying to address the concerns of my villagers and used to share his strategies for safeguarding the community. I can still recall one such meeting in which he passionately conveyed the importance of unity and vigilance in confronting the threat of dacoits, motivating the villagers to stand together in solidarity.

2. **Non-Verbal Communication:** Ramdas was an expert in expressions to convey empathy, resolve people's concerns, and, above all, demonstrate determination. He used to walk up to people; sometimes, he used to pat on their backs, and other times, he used to put his hand on people's shoulders to comfort them in times of panic. He was always successful in instilling confidence and trust through his non-verbal cues.

3. **Written Communication:** I am a great admirer of Ramdas. During a time when resources were limited, and many villagers were uneducated, he designed

several posters that outlined safety protocols and emergency procedures, complete with pictures. School and college students were asked to distribute handwritten pamphlets with clear messages to various groups. These posters and pamphlets were tangible reminders of the community's collective commitment to safety, empowering villagers with essential information even in Ramdas' absence. They were beneficial to the villagers.

4. **Visual Communication:** Champion Ramdas was known for creating beautiful murals on blackboards in my school. He depicted scenes of unity, resilience, and defiance against the threats of dacoits. Ramdas encouraged young boys and girls to copy and paint on the walls of their homes, which served as a powerful symbol of hope and inspiration for all who passed by.

With his efforts, Ramdas could engage the villagers effectively and inspire others to do the same. He even became a trainer to many, and his message spread like wildfire. Other nearby villages sought his help, and Ramdas was happy to accept and train their proposals.

Today, I can add a few more methods and advise Ramdas to be even more effective.

A- **Demonstrative Communication:** I suggest that Ramdas organize practical demonstrations of self-defense techniques and emergency response drills. This will enable villagers to participate actively and learn from their own experiences. By doing so, Ramdas can empower the villagers to take proactive measures against potential threats.

B- **Digital Communication:** Today, Ramdas can quickly establish a communication network using digital platforms, such as text messaging, or form social media groups to share real-time updates.

I want to summarize effective communication from Ramdas' point of view.

Effective communication is the art of accurately and persuasively conveying messages while listening actively and empathetically to others. Let me share the key elements of effective communication.

Clarity: Effective communication begins with clear and concise expression. The message should be easy to understand, and there should be no scope for ambiguity for the audience.

Active Listening: Active listening is an integral part of communication. Today, it is more in demand and less in supply. People don't want to listen.

Empathy: Empathy is about understanding the emotions and perspectives of others. Validating others' feelings helps build trust and strong interpersonal relations.

Feedback: Feedback is essential for gauging understanding and ensuring message clarity. Always encourage open and constructive feedback. You can foster a culture of continuous learning and mutual respect.

Nonverbal clues, Such as body language, facial expressions, and tone of voice, play a significant role in communication.

Adaptability: Effective communicators adapt their communication style to suit the needs and preferences of their audience. Flexibility makes them more effective.

Respect: Treat others with dignity and courtesy. Be considerate of them; some people may take more time to understand your message, so show respect to them and accept them as they are.

Purposeful Communication: Your Communication must be purposeful and goal-oriented. Define the objective very clearly. Select channels with care so you can maximize the impact and effectiveness of your communication efforts.

Conflict Resolution: If there is a team and teamwork, then conflict is bound to exist. Effective communication is instrumental in resolving conflicts and addressing differences constructively. Open dialogue, active listening, and collaboration facilitate the negotiation of solutions, and harmony can be restored very soon.

Continuous Improvement: Be a lifelong learner. Have a growth mindset. You can improve your communication skills through practice, feedback, and self-reflection. Be an effective communicator in various contexts.

My suggestion: Master these elements to convey your message with impact, build meaningful connections, and foster positive relationships in personal and professional settings.

Key Elements: Clarity, Active Listening, Empathy, feedback, awareness of nonverbal cues, adaptability, respect, purposefulness, conflict resolution, and commitment to improvement

PRINCIPLES OF EFFECTIVE COMMUNICATION

"To effectively communicate, we must realize that we are all different in how we perceive the world and use this understanding to guide our communication with others."

- Tony Robbins

I learned a lot from my school headmaster during my childhood. Those learning from my headmaster, the wisdom of my father, and the curiosity of Ramdas have helped me throughout my life, and I am feeling so happy to share those learnings with you with more gratitude to all those persons; I am and will remain indebted in my life.

My headmaster shared a story about Mulla Nasreddin's wise silence one day.

Once, Mulla Nasreddin was invited to the Sultan's court to offer his wisdom on governance matters. Sitting among the courtiers, the Sultan posed a challenging question to test the Mulla's wit.

Tell me, Mulla, "The Sultan inquired," what is the secret of effective communication?"

The courtiers eagerly leaned in, but Nasreddin remained silent with a mischievous grin.

The Sultan, puzzled by Mulla's silence, pressed him for an explanation. Why do you remain silent, Mulla? Do you have nothing to say on the matter?"

With a twinkle in his eyes, Nasreddin replied, "Your majesty, I believe the most profound lessons are often conveyed not through words but through actions—or inactions, in this case."

The Sultan and his courtiers exchanged perplexed glances, unsure of the Mulla's intentions. Sensing their confusion, Nasreddin continued, "Effective communication is not always about speaking, Your Majesty; it is about when to speak and when to listen, when to convey messages directly and when to allow silence to speak volumes."

The court laughed at Naserddin's clever response, and the Sultan pondered the lesson in silence, impressed by the Mulla's wisdom.

I came from my school to home and was excited to share this story with my father. He listened to the story attentively, and Ramdas joined us in between. After listening to me, he suggested that I finish my lunch and come with my key learnings. Honestly, I was not very happy as I was in a mood to play with my friends, but I had no option.

I invite you to list your key lessons from this story.

1.

2.

3.

4.

If I have to share my key learnings today, then I would like to list them as follows-

Sometimes, the most effective communication is silence. Silence allows for reflection, introspection, and the space for others to express themselves. "Feel the power of silence."

Knowing when to speak and when to listen is essential for effective communication. Gauging the appropriate moment to convey messages for maximum impact is vital. "Timing is Key."

Humor can be a powerful tool for conveying messages and insights. Such learnings remain with you for a long. You can engage your audience for a long with your humor. "Use Humour as a teaching tool."

Effective communication encompasses more than just verbal communication; nonverbal cues, actions, and even silence can convey messages and meanings. "You can communicate Beyond Words"

After sharing my key learnings, my father appreciated my efforts. Ramdas also shared a few of his points and asked his Guru Ji (My father), Guru Ji, what we should remember while communicating with others. It also sounded exciting, and I decided to listen to their conversations with a very positive frame of mind.

Guru Ji, with a familiar smile, said, Ramdas, not as a rule but as a Principle, you should keep following things in mind. As a curious boy, I asked my father to give me clarity about **what rules and principles are.**

As per his nature, my father said, "Treat others as you would like to be treated." And asked us to share our understanding.

I learned in childhood that this principle, often called the Golden Rule, guides behavior by prompting empathy and respect for others. My father taught us the rules and principles.

If specific guidelines dictate a particular action, it is a Rule.

Rules are typically rigid and leave little room for interpretation or flexibility.

There is a clear consequence for non-compliance with a rule.

Ex-"Speed limit on this highway is 60 miles per hour."- as we can see, specific directives must be followed, and failure means- Fine, I mean Penalty.

Principle: A principle is a fundamental truth or guideline that informs decision-making and behavior. Principles help people navigate complex situations and adapt to changing circumstances.

Example- Treat others as you would like to be treated. He asked us if we see any specific action suggested here in this example. We were still waiting for a response. What is your response?

Yes, you are right; there is no suggestion for any specific action. However, there is encouragement for individuals to consider the impact of their behavior on others.

Remember, rules and principles play essential roles in guiding behavior and decision-making, but they operate at different levels of specificity and flexibility.

Please note your understanding and your example.

At Ramdas's insistence, his Guru Ji continued to help us understand the fundamental principle of effective communication. To teach us a lesson I can recall even today, was that powerful. Let me share the example he gave. Please read the following statement carefully.

"To actualize optimizing resource utilization, we must enhance our synergy paradigm by implementing proactive strategies."

What does this statement look like?

Sophisticated? Simple? Complex? Or sophisticated due to the use of jargon and complex phrasing.

So Ramdas asked his Guru Ji what the message was in this sentence. As usual, with a smile, Guru Ji said, Dear Ramdas, the underlying message is relatively straightforward. With curiosity, we both asked together what that was.

He said the message is-"**We need to work together more efficiently.**"

I learned the first principle of effective communication: Clarity. The message should be clear, concise, and easy to understand without unnecessary jargon, ambiguity, or overly complicated language.

I used 2nd learning in my professional life, which was very effective. For ex-

"Increase sales by 10% next quarter"

Think briefly and note that this sentence conveys a clear and specific directive in just six words. There is no unnecessary detail or elaboration.

My learning was- "**Conciseness.**"

Another thing I learned from such interactions was based on the situation, story, and other experiences I shared.

Let me share one such incident here with us.

One day, Guru Ji asked Ramdas about his non-availability in the village for many days. He narrated a story about the loss of a close family member of his wife. Guru Ji listened to him for a long time without any interruption or passing judgment. Once he finished, he said two sentences only.

I can understand your emotions, Ramdas.

If there's anything I can do to support you during this time, please do not hesitate to let me know.

In my books, I have shared a few heart-touching life experiences of my friends.

My learnings were "**Active Listening** and **Empathy**."

Effective listening means giving full attention, nodding to show understanding, paraphrasing to ensure comprehension, and asking open-ended questions. By practicing effective listening, you can create an environment where team members feel heard and valued.

Empathy means offering genuine support and compassion. Avoid judgment and provide continued support. If you can comfort someone during difficult times, you can foster trust and connection in a relationship.

Respect: Treat everyone with respect, courtesy, and professionalism. It reminds me of one of the situations in my village. We were preparing for the Holi festival celebration, and a junior member gave an idea that was not in line with the festivities; someone from us shouted at him, and this young boy could not understand what was happening. Ramdas managed the situation well and explained to the gentleman shouting at the young boy. He said you may disagree with his idea, but instead of immediately dismissing his idea, you should have listened to the boy who was enthusiastic to participate in the event. You might have also killed his motivation to participate actively in future events. Ramdas's suggestion to the group was straightforward. First, thank you for your ideas and suggestions. You then express your thoughts respectfully. By showing respect, you are protecting his self-esteem and encouraging him to participate with better thoughts and ideas in the future. By this simple gesture, you can foster an environment of mutual respect and collaboration. I learned a good lesson early and practiced it in my life.

There was more learning from those festivities and people's involvement. Time and technology are changing fast. Be ready to accept these changes and adapt to new situations. When I started my career in sales, there were traditional selling methods, and we enjoyed those methods and were successful. Over some time, those methods could have been more effective in the rapidly evolving market. With time, I realized that the competition and consumer preferences have changed. I realized that I needed to adapt to survive. Embrace openness to new ideas and approaches. Ask for help from your seniors, mentor them, attend webinars, read books, and experiment with innovative sales techniques.

Remember: "There are endless possibilities and opportunities for growth." If you want to thrive, be open to new ideas and flexible.

So my learnings were "**Openness and adaptability.**"

Recently, I met one of my college friends who had experienced many ups and downs in his life. He lost his father in his childhood. At a very early age, he started a business with the help of his uncle. I inquired about his journey and asked what has made you a successful businessman. His one-liner response was, "**Consistent approach to business practices.**"

I was impressed with his response and was very happy to see him flourishing in his life after a long struggle. He shared with me the following-

At the beginning of my journey as a businessman, I established clear goals and developed a strategic plan with the help of my uncle. My focus was on the execution of the plan. I kept reminding my team about my goals by maintaining regular communication with my team. As a result of his consistency, my friend established a loyal customer base. His business grew steadily, and he could achieve sustainable success despite the challenges and uncertainties in his life. I could feel the confidence in his eyes, the solid foundation for long-term growth and prosperity. And my learning is **"Consistency."**

Remember: "Consistent communication builds trust and credibility over time."

You might have seen many failures due to needing more consistency in your surroundings.

I'll be happy to help you with that. Here's the revised text:

One of my neighbors was a fitness enthusiast who had set a goal to exercise regularly and maintain a healthy diet. His family also supported his efforts, as he was a little overweight. Initially, he was highly motivated and diligently followed his exercise routine and diet. However, over time, he began to slack off and skipped workouts while inconsistently indulging in unhealthy eating habits. As a result of his inconsistency, he could have seen significant progress in his fitness goals. His energy levels were low, and he struggled to maintain his desired weight. His fitness journey became an uphill battle without consistency in his efforts, ultimately failing to achieve the desired outcomes.

As seen in the above examples, consistency is pivotal in determining outcomes. In contrast, the lack of consistency leads to failure and frustration.

Remember: "Consistency fosters success and resilience." 'Consistency allows you to stay focused, build momentum, and achieve your goals effectively.'

Let us talk about Active listening and the role of active listening in communication.

ACTIVE LISTENING

'Use your eyes and your ears'- "If you make listening and observation your occupation, you will gain much more than you can by talk."

- Robert Barden–Powell, Boy Scouts Association

Remember- Listening is a sign of respect.

We all know that active listening is a fundamental component of effective communication; still, you find people around you who believe in telling and not listening. Active listening involves hearing spoken words and understanding the underlying message, emotions, and perspectives. It requires focus, empathy, and a genuine desire to comprehend and connect with the speaker.

Why genuine desire- Because desires are generally weak, and they need support, support of dedication, determination, and discipline.

Active listening is crucial in communication, enhancing understanding, building rapport, and fostering meaningful connections between team members. Active listening can do wonders for a leader. Let me remind you about the water problem in my village and how Ramdas helped villagers overcome that problem permanently in my previous episodes. It is time to share a scene from that day's discussion. Many people actively participated in the discussion. Ramdas led the discussion, and my father moderated the proceedings. There was tremendous excitement, especially among children my age, as we imagined hot summers and ponds with water to comfort all of us.

Full of excitement, Ramdas begins to share the project. But before he can finish his opening remarks, one senior member interrupts him, eager to share his concerns and experience. This gentleman fails to notice the disappointment in Ramdas's eyes. This is a common scenario around us almost every day. Is there any solution to such problems? Yes, active listening offers a remedy to this all-too-common communication pitfall.

Active listening requires attentiveness, empathy, and a genuine desire to understand the other's perspective.

My father noticed that many people were interested in seeking advice from Ramdas. He decided to manage the situation by asking everyone to take a break and come up with their ideas and suggestions the next day so the meeting could be more meaningful. Disappointed, Ramdas asked my father, "Guru Ji, what should I do in this case?"

My father (Guru Ji) took Ramdas near the pond and asked him to bring a stone from his bag. The stone was engraved with ancient symbols and was known as the Wisdom Stone. It held the wisdom of generations past. Everyone was excited to know more about this stone. It was not an ordinary stone as it had power in it. Anyone who held this stone to their ear and closed their eyes could hear the whispers of the villagers through the ages - their joys, sorrows, and aspirations echoing through the ages.

Everyone was interested in experiencing that excitement. The voices of his fellow villagers deeply moved Ramdas, and he realized the importance of active listening to understand their needs and foster harmony within the community. From that moment on, Ramdas carried the Wisdom stone with him wherever he went, reminding him of the importance of active listening and empathetic leadership. Ramdas was seeking the advice of his Guru Ji. I suggest you get such advice as a wisdom of the stone from your mentor or leader to become a beacon of light in your organization. Ramdas became a beacon in my village, leading by example and inspiring others to embrace the values of compassion, understanding, and unity.

Learning: The story of Ramdas and Wisdom Stone highlights the transformative power of active listening and empathetic leadership. We should listen attentively to the voices of our teams; this will help foster trust, understanding, and harmony.

EXERCISE

Why should we listen attentively to others?

Remember when following a rule or principle influenced your behavior or decision-making?

Let us further understand whether active listening has any role in communication.

ROLE OF ACTIVE LISTENING IN COMMUNICATION

"Most people do not listen with the intent to understand; they listen with the intent to reply."

- Stephen R. Covey

Stephen R. Covey says that nicely and is so true to the above. In the previous chapter, we have seen this happening in real life.

Today, we live in a world where everyone seems to be talking; no one is willing to listen. We all know that authentic communication begins with the art of listening. Active listening is about understanding the emotions, intentions, and nuances behind them. By embracing the power of active listening, we can foster deeper connections, resolve conflicts, and build trust in our relationships. It's time to shift our focus from speaking to truly understanding—to listen with our ears, hearts, and minds.

There are many vital roles of active listening. Let us discuss a few of them here.

Building Trust and Respect: I understand that you have many personal experiences that you can draw upon. Trust and rapport can be established when you perceive your leader attentively listening to and comprehending your viewpoints. This forms the foundation of open and sincere communication, strengthening interpersonal relationships between you and your leader.

Enhancing Comprehension: Active listening is an essential skill that allows you to hear, comprehend, and process your thoughts. When you actively listen, you pay attention to verbal and nonverbal cues, which help you better understand the speaker's perspective. This understanding enables you to respond more effectively and interact better with others.

Facilitating Problem-solving and Conflict Resolution: Active listening promotes collaboration and problem-solving by encouraging open sharing of concerns and perspectives. By improving your listening skills, you will have the time to identify common ground, explore alternative solutions, and resolve conflict effectively.

Empowering Others: Active listening is a great skill to learn. Improving this skill allows you to express yourself freely and feel valued for your contributions. You can create a supportive environment where everyone's voice is heard and respected. Active listening can improve your confidence, making your approach more creative and innovative.

Improving Leadership and Team Dynamics: Great leaders understand the importance of being good listeners and recommend developing active listening as a core leadership skill. Active listening helps build trust, foster collaboration, and motivate team members. These leaders listen to receive feedback and understand their team members' needs. They are skilled at inspiring, engaging, driving performance, and cultivating a positive work culture.

Remember: Active listening is a crucial aspect of effective communication. It helps develop understanding, empathy, and a deeper connection among team members. By improving your active listening skills, you can enhance your relationships, resolve conflicts, and achieve tremendous success in your personal and professional life.

The art of telling and listening—Effective communication involves clearly expressing ourselves and actively listening to others. As an effective leader, you should master these skills.

Art of Telling- **Consider the power of storytelling** when it comes to telling. Imagine a sales meeting where a skilled presenter weaves a narrative that resonates with the team, gets the attention of his team members, and can ignite their imagination. This will help you convey your message about either the process or the product and elicit their emotions to foster connections. You will achieve your goal- to encourage your team members to take action.

Art of Listening- Imagine a scenario where you actively listen during a team meeting. As team members voice their concerns and ideas, you demonstrate genuine interest, maintain eye contact, and nod in acknowledgment.

'Always paraphrase key points and ask clarifying questions.' This will continually improve your understanding and validation, building trust within the team.

So far, we have seen the fundamentals of active listening, its role in communication, and how it helps build relationships and achieve tremendous success. Let us discuss empathy in our next chapter.

EMPATHY

"Empathy is the opposite of spiritual meanness. It's the capacity to understand that every war is won and lost. And that someone else's pain is as meaningful as your own."

- ***Barbara Kingsolver***

Take a moment to reflect on when you felt honestly heard and understood by another person. I asked one of my friends this question during an informal gathering of old colleagues. After much struggle, he could say that perhaps his college friend listened without judgment. As we were talking on this subject, he shared another name of one of his professional colleagues who was taking the time to empathize with him during his struggle in those moments. My friend became a little serious while discussing things among ourselves, though it was an informal kind of gathering, so thoughts flowed freely. We are so busy in our daily routines, and we forget that there exists a profound power—the power of empathy and active listening. These twin pillars of communication serve as the bedrock of genuine connections, fostering understanding, compassion, and meaningful relationships in a world too often full of misunderstanding and discord.

We see that everybody is in a hurry, and there are distractions and divided attention; the art of empathy and active listening is at risk of being overshadowed. We are quick to respond and busy formulating rather than genuinely understanding the words and emotions conveyed. Another friend from the group admitted that we are rushing to offer solutions without fully grasping the depth of another person's experience. Do we need a different mindset grounded in empathy and active listening?

What if we consciously tried to set aside our preconceptions and connect with others on a deeper level? Asked another friend.

It was amicable, and we explored the transformative power of empathy and active listening in our personal and professional lives. Based on those interactions, we will deep dive into the science behind these practices, uncovering the neurological and psychological mechanisms that nurture our ability to empathize and engage with others. We will try to find ways and practical strategies for cultivating empathy and sharpening our active listening skills.

"Empathy is the starting point for creating a community and taking action. It's the impetus for creating change."- Max Carver.

So, let us embark on this journey together- a journey into the heart of connection, where empathy and active listening serve as our guiding lights, illuminating the path toward more meaningful and fulfilling relationships.

Remember: "Active listening is a skill anyone can learn."

Neurological Mechanism: research has revealed that specific brain regions are activated when we engage in active listening and empathetic interactions. The prefrontal cortex, responsible for higher-order thinking and decision-making, is crucial in processing social cues, understanding other's perspectives, and regulating our emotional responses. Meanwhile, the putative mirror neuron system, located in the brain's motor cortex, fires when we observe other's actions and emotions, allowing us to vicariously experience their feelings and intentions.

Psychologically, empathy is shaped by a complex interplay of cognitive and affective factors. Cognitive empathy involves understanding and taking perspective, whereas affective empathy involves sharing and resonating with others' emotions. Together, these components enable us to form deep connections and emotional bonds with others, fostering a sense of belonging and mutual understanding.

By understanding the neurological and psychological underpinnings of empathy and active listening, we gain insight into why these practices are essential for building meaningful relationships and fostering a sense of empathy and understanding in our interactions with others.

Disclaimer: The information above about the neuroscience and psychology underlying empathy and active listening is based on current scientific understanding and research findings. While efforts have been made to represent this information accurately, I encourage you to consult relevant scholarly sources for further exploration and verification.

We have discussed the role of active listening in communication and understood that this is a crucial skill that anyone can develop. We know this skill is related to active listening and will take time to develop. Start practicing to develop this skill. Active listening will make you a better professional and good human being.

Remember: "Practice makes things permanent."

What should be practiced to help improve active listening?

I would like to suggest a few practical tips that will enhance your active listening skills-

Give Your Full Attention: This world is full of distractions, so you should eliminate distractions and give the speaker your full attention. When conversing with your team or team leaders, maintain eye contact and use a few words like "I see" or Please "Carry On." This shows your engagement.

Practice Empathy: This is crucial. I suggest paying attention to the speaker's words, tone of voice, facial expression, and body language to grasp their emotions and feelings better. How can you do that? Is it that simple? Yes, it is! Just try to put yourself in the speaker's shoes and understand his perspective.

Try- not Interrupting: sometimes, you are urged to interrupt your thoughts or opinions while the speaker is talking. Let him express himself fully before responding. You will learn better; try next time- avoid interrupting.

Sometimes, we are carried away with our thoughts and may need to put our viewpoints and jump in with our opinions and suggestions. Don't worry; we will get more time and contribute more and better. How?

Paraphrase and Reflect: Wait, let the speaker finish his talk, and paraphrase what he said to ensure you have understood correctly. Reflect on his main points to show you've been actively listening and to clarify any misunderstandings.

"Empathy represents the foundation skill for all the social competencies important for work."- Daniel Goleman.

For example, one of my experiences is a routine appraisal meeting with a pharma company's junior manager (Rohan). The senior manager(Mr Gupta) was having a one-on-one meeting. Rohan expresses frustration about feeling overwhelmed with his workload and struggling to meet deadlines. Now, there are two scenarios, and I am sharing both these scenarios with you-

A. Mr Gupta - "Well. Have you tried prioritizing your tasks better? Maybe you should work on managing your time more efficiently."

B. Mr Gupta - "It sounds like you're feeling stressed, but by how much work you must do. Can you tell me more about the tasks causing you the most difficulty?"

If you are Mr Gupta, which one is your choice?

Decided?

Let me share my point first.

In the first scenario, Mr. Gupta responds to Rohan's concern with a solution without fully understanding the underlying issues. Imagine you are Rohan- This can make you

feel unheard and dismissed, leading to frustration and resentment. Yes or No?

In the second scenario, Mr Gupta paraphrases and reflects on Rohan's concerns about him. Do you agree with my point? If yes, Mr Gupta validates his feelings and encourages him to elaborate on his challenges.

You will agree that this demonstrates active listening and empathy, fostering a more open and productive conversation.

Now, what is your choice? Scenario No.1 or 2?

If you choose Scenario No. 2, you will understand that this encourages trust, strengthens relationships, and fosters a supportive and collaborative environment where individuals feel valued and respected.

Remember: Paraphrasing and reflecting are essential communication skills that promote understanding, validation, and empathy.

Always ask Open-ended questions: This is the art of asking a question that shows you genuinely understand the speaker's perspective and encourages deeper conversation.

Open-ended questions start with either 'H' or any of the 'W,' which means' How,' ' What,' ' Why,' ' When,' and' Where.' They need more explanation and can not be answered 'Yes or No.' For example, I would like to ask If you enjoyed the team-building activity.

The question does not start with 'H' or 'W' and can quickly be answered with 'Yes or No.' Therefore, it is not open-ended.

There is a risk of ending the conversation quickly. You will get limited information only.

On the other hand, the open-ended question, "What were your thoughts on the team-building activity?" how do you think it could be improved?" invites the individual to share their opinions, insights, and suggestions in more detail. This technique encourages deeper reflection and discussion, fostering a more meaningful and productive exchange of ideas.

Remember: BY asking open-ended questions, we can promote deeper understanding, uncover new ideas, and build stronger connections with others.

Be in the Present: Many people start thinking of another world while the speaker is still speaking, and they start implementing his ideas. Let go of distractions and fully immerse yourself in the interaction with the speaker.

Request feedback: Don't hesitate to ask for feedback on your active listening skills. Start with your friends, family, and colleagues, and they will give you valuable insights and suggestions for improvement.

Reflect on your conversation: Reflect on your interactions and identify areas where you could have been a more active listener. Learn from your experiences and strive to improve in future conversations.

Be patient with yourself: Learning any new skill takes time, and active listening skills are no exception. So, be patient with yourself as you improve. Celebrate your progress and continue to challenge yourself to become a better listener.

Remember: "Active listening is not just about hearing words—it's about understanding, empathy, and building meaningful relationships through communication."

Let me refresh our discussions on active listening. Active listening is a powerful skill that enhances communication, fosters understanding, and strengthens relationships. We can create a more supportive and collaborative environment where everyone feels valued and heard by giving our full attention, demonstrating empathy, and reflecting on what others say.

EXERCISE

Take a moment to reflect on a recent conversation with someone- a friend, family member, or colleague. Think about how well you listened during that conversation. Were you entirely present, or were you distracted by your thoughts? Did you actively engage with the speaker, or did you find yourself formulating your thoughts?

Write down three key points from the conversation and consider how you could have listened more effectively.

Then, challenge yourself to apply these insights in your future interactions, striving to be a more attentive and empathetic listener.

Let us discuss persuasion in the next chapter. What is persuasion, and what is its role in active listening?

PERSUASION

"Pretend that everyone you meet has a sign on his or her neck that says, 'Make me feel important.' Not only will you succeed in sales, you will succeed in life."

*- **Mary Kay Ash***

WHAT IS PERSUASION?

Persuasion influences someone's attitude, beliefs, or behaviors through communication and reasoning.

What is the role of persuasion in communication?

Persuasion is crucial in building rapport, fostering understanding, and facilitating constructive dialogue.

How does persuasion function within the context of active listening?

Before discussing how persuasion functions, let us understand why building rapport is essential.

As you are already in a leadership role, you know the importance of rapport building, and those who are future leaders, let them understand a few reasons.

Establishing Trust is the no one reason – building rapport creates a foundation of trust between communicators. When individuals feel connected, they are more likely to be open, honest, and receptive to one another's ideas and perspectives.

Improving understanding is another reason- Rapport facilitates better understanding between communicators. Individuals are more willing to listen attentively, ask questions, and clarify misunderstandings when there is a sense of mutual respect and rapport.

Reducing conflict is another reason- conflict and misunderstanding are part of communication and are bound to be there as individuals have their views on a subject. So, it is vital to understand that when there is a positive rapport between the team and team leader, they are more likely to approach disagreements with respect and empathy. It is seen in the team where there is respect and empathy, and they have better problem-solving abilities.

I have seen the benefits of building rapport go beyond professional life and are long-lasting.

So, start to build rapport with your team. This will lay the groundwork for trust, understanding, collaboration, engagement, conflict resolution, and positive relationships, all crucial for effective communication and interpersonal dynamics.

STORYTIME

On a cold and rainy day, I took refuge in a quaint tea shop in a busy marketplace. I unexpectedly reunited with an old acquaintance I hadn't seen in 25 years. As we sipped our hot drinks, my friend shared a poignant tale of his journey and the invaluable lessons he learned along the way.

My friend grew up in a comfortable home with working parents who loved and cared for him. However, his aspirations were shaped by something other than his family's surroundings but by the neighboring family's affluence and prestige. As a result, he veered off course, seeking validation from neighbors instead of focusing on his studies. Despite his parents' concern, his mother remained supportive while his father's dream for him unraveled.

Misunderstanding further complicated my friend's journey when a conversation with his uncle (neighbor) about plans led him down a misguided path. He chose a career that diverged from his father's wishes and became a salesperson in an FMCG company. But the demands of the job and his personal life soon took their toll. He struggled with stress and dissatisfaction, which led him to an unhealthy coping mechanism, causing him to miss out on opportunities and regret his choices.

Despite the setbacks, my friend's family remained a source of strength. His wife's unwavering support and his son's achievements were beacons of hope in turbulent times. Reflecting on his journey, my friend shared his regrets and pleaded with others to learn from his missteps. He emphasized the importance of staying true to one's priorities, fostering clear communication, maintaining a healthy work-life balance, and embracing resilience in the face of adversity. He did not listen to his uncle's voice, made the wrong decision, and suffered greatly.

If I had to ask you your take-home points from this story about my friends, what would they be?

I suggest the following to you as my key points.

A. Always prioritize your Goals.

B. Communication and Understanding- be a good listener first and always ask for clarity. Miscommunication and assumptions can lead to significant misunderstandings. In this case, my friend misinterpreted his uncle's intentions.

C. Balancing work and personal life- is crucial for overall well-being and happiness.

Remember- Wrong guesses are very costly.

Exercise: Have you ever found yourself prioritizing the expectations or desires of others over your own goals and aspirations?

How did this impact your decisions and outcomes?

Think momentarily and identify when miscommunication or assumptions led to misunderstanding or regrets.

How did you overcome these challenges?

1984, Dr. Robert B. Cialdini published six Persuasion principles in his book Influence: The Psychology of

Persuasion. This is one of the most famous books available in 26 languages and is still as relevant today as in 1984.

I am sharing these principles with you here.

1. Reciprocity
2. Commitment and Consistency
3. Social Proof
4. Authority
5. Liking
6. Scarcity

Dr Cialdini compiled these simple principles based on his research. Let's discuss how we can apply them to our personal and professional lives.

1. Reciprocity- How do you feel when you do something for someone without expecting anything in return? This principle is all about psychology, and I am sure your answer is, 'I will be happy, or I feel good.' It is also experienced by all of us when we do something for others, and they are more likely to do something for us in the future. This is called reciprocity, and remember- this is not about exchanging favors but rather about giving freely without any condition attached.

2. Commitment and Consistency—Studies have shown that people tend to behave consistently with their past actions, even unconsciously. Can you recall a few of

your personal experiences? Let me remind you about likes on social media platforms. If someone likes your post, they want to do something other than perform an enormous favor later with your comments.

3. Social Proof- "Let me ask you a question: if you were out for dinner with your family, and there were two restaurants in the area - one crowded and another almost empty - which would you choose? I'm sure your answer would be the crowded restaurant over the almost empty one. We all know the service may be slower in a crowded restaurant, but popularity is key. Let me give one more example: When making any purchase, you tend to look for reviews first, not just to satisfy yourself, but also as a form of social proof."

4. Authority- we tend to give deference to those in positions of power or authority, such as Professors, Doctors, and experts in various fields. Before choosing to purchase a car, whom do you consult or follow opinion, your neighbor or an expert? It happens subconsciously, and you are likely to give more weight to the opinions of those with more power or expertise. This concept is similar to social proof, but rather than being based on numbers, it is based on perceived authority.

5. Liking- Successful salespeople understand the importance of building rapport before diving into business. Multiple studies have shown that we tend to be more influenced by individuals who share

similarities, such as background, personality, or social status. Research on negotiations has shown that individuals who establish common ground and exchange personal information are 90% more likely to agree. Next time, when you are doing persuasion with someone, focus on building rapport and developing relationships. Try to find common interests. Star performers pay compliments, establish connections, and strive to be friendly with their clients or prospects.

6. Scarcity—One of persuasion's fundamental principles is highlighting the scarcity or rarity of a product or service. Human beings tend to value things that are limited or in short supply. Words such as "exclusive" and "limited edition" tend to create a perception of higher value. Research has shown that labeling a product with a limited supply can increase its perceived value and the likelihood of purchase.

Word of caution- genuine scarcity is different than manufacturing it.

Can scarcity improve my Reputation?

The scarcity principle, used for ages in persuasion, can also enhance your reputation. How? When others perceive you as scarce, they naturally assign more excellent value to you. Right?

Do you think this elevated worth will amplify your persuasive influence and help you achieve your goals?

Not only this, but scarcity can also cultivate admiration and respect from your team members. You can create differentiation for yourself and can become noteworthy.

Word of caution- avoid excessive portrayal of scarcity.

Dr. Robert Cialdini's six principles of persuasion explain what compels people to say 'yes.' These principles are well-supported by psychology studies and are used in fields like sales and marketing.

I have seen that Dr Cialdini's Principles of persuasion are helpful in

Increase trust

Create a better image of a brand

And inspire people to take action.

I suggest applying these principles with ethics in mind and avoiding manipulation.

I suggest trying these persuasive techniques in your field. You will increase trust and credibility with your clients and prospects.

FOSTERING MEANINGFUL CONNECTIONS

"Communication leads to community, that is, understanding intimacy, and mutual valuing."

- Rollo May

STORYTIME

The following experience was shared by one of my chemist friends. In his own words-

In the early 90s, I ran a chemist shop when a customer visited with a unique problem. He complained that his wife had impaired hearing and asked for a remedy. I advised him to consult with a leading consultant, but he insisted on a hearing aid and asked about the cost. I referred him to a reliable person for that. Before he left, I asked how he knew his wife had impaired hearing. He told me that she wasn't responding to his questions, so I suggested he test her hearing ability again that day, and I would refer him to a consultant for further investigation the next day.

The following day, he shared an exciting episode with me. When he came home, he asked his wife from the door, "Honey, I am back home. What's for dinner tonight?" There was no response, so he repeated the question twice, getting no response either time. He then went further into the house and repeated the question, this time with a louder voice. Finally, his wife replied boomingly, "This is the fourth time I'm telling you, it's Veg Pizza!"

I was shocked by this experience and felt terrible for the poor lady's luck. This gentleman was a big-time miser and asked if he could get an economical hearing aid. Understanding his approach, I put a string around his neck and said, "Just put this button in your ear and stick this string in your pocket." When he asked how it worked, I said, "It doesn't work. But if people see it on you, they will speak louder, and you will save all your money!

I learned a lesson that day, and my key learnings are as follows:

Importance of communication- Effective communication is significant in understanding and addressing issues.

Creative Problem-Solving—The chemist's makeshift solution demonstrates the power of creative problem-solving. Sometimes, unconventional approaches can yield effective results, especially when faced with constraints or limitations.

Keen Observation helped the chemist discern the true nature of my customer's problem.

Humor and Light-heartedness—Humor can often diffuse tense situations and foster connection. The chemist's light-hearted approach provided fun and helped alleviate the customer's concern.

Financial Prudence- The customer's frugality highlights the importance of being mindful of expenses and seeking cost-effective solutions. It prompts us to consider alternatives and prioritize financial prudence in decision-making.

My take-home message- "Approach challenges with an open mind, a sense of humor, and a willingness to think outside the box."

Effective communication begins with active listening. Listening is not about hearing words but about genuinely understanding others' perspectives.

"Advice I got from my Mentor at the beginning of my journey as a leader."

"Put yourself in the shoes of a speaker to understand their emotions, fears, and desires. At the beginning of my leadership journey, my coach advised me not to be quick to provide solutions. Instead, I should empathetically listen to my team members, acknowledge their feelings, and validate their experiences.

Sometimes, nonverbal cues say more than words. I suggest studying body language and paying attention to participants' facial expressions. Unsaid thoughts can speak volumes. This reminds me of a team meeting where a young manager hesitated to speak, but I could read in his eyes that he had something to say. After the meeting, I called him to my hotel room and gave him space to express himself over coffee.

During the meeting, we discussed activities for the next financial year, including brand strategy, brand awareness campaigns, patient education, and CRM.

Many suggestions were made, and ensuring everyone could be heard was essential." "Put yourself in the shoes of a speaker to understand their emotions, fears, and desires. At the beginning of my leadership journey, my coach advised me not to be quick to provide solutions. Instead, I should empathetically listen to my team members, acknowledge their feelings, and validate their experiences.

Pay attention to nonverbal cues such as body language and facial expressions, as they can often convey more information than words. During a team meeting, I noticed a young manager who seemed hesitant to speak.

However, I could tell from the look in his eyes that he had something important to say. Realizing he needed a supportive environment, I invited him to my hotel room after the meeting and offered him a coffee. During our conversation, he freely shared his opinions, perspectives, and experience with CRM from his previous company.

This young manager's insights helped me make better decisions and solve problems more effectively. I suggest you practice such constructive and respectful dialogue with those who have different or even opposite views, which are value-based. Once you give them a supportive environment, they feel comfortable and valued that their voice is heard. Creating such situations has benefits and challenges, but better options are always available.

BENEFITS

By seeking out the views and perspectives of others, we can better understand their opinions and develop a sense of respect for individuals. Through this process, we can learn about the assumptions made when making a particular decision and what is expected from individuals. I have benefited from this approach, leading to an improved workplace atmosphere of appreciation and better presentations. Additionally, I have reduced my biases and provided a supportive environment by listening to people with different views.

Critical thinking and Creativity—I want to share my experience with you. The first time I invited my manager to have a private discussion with me, it allowed me to think from various angles before inviting him. I questioned and answered myself, which helped me improve my reasoning and analysis and got many new and innovative ideas. Later in my career, this became my way of life, and my team improved significantly.

The first person with such an opportunity had many inhibitions and feared rejection. However, he was able to develop a sense of belonging and inclusion. Later, it became a routine for me, and my team had better teamwork, cooperation, and trust.

Challenges- I faced some challenges initially as people were anxious, defensive, and resistant to expressing themselves. However, it takes courage and openness from both you and your team members to overcome these obstacles. It's important to be ready to take risks and learn from mistakes, as it's natural to make mistakes initially.

When managing critical moments, it's essential to recognize that team members may have different levels of knowledge, interest, and engagement in discussions. To handle such situations, I followed a simple principle of setting clear rules for the participants. For example, I explained the purpose of the goals and the meeting to avoid misunderstandings. I always suggested that team members be honest and fair and participate with openness and trust within the boundaries we set.

I used these opportunities to learn, so I was always respectful towards my team members. I never interrupted them, tried to dominate the discussion, or dismissed any of their ideas initially. I was very attentive while listening to them.

When they disagreed, I expressed my views and values clearly but respectfully. How? I practiced this simple technique: first, acknowledge and appreciate their views and values. Then, ask questions and seek clarification from them. I never criticized their views and avoided being judgmental.

I took such situations as a great platform to learn. Sometimes, I also changed my views and was always open and curious.

Keywords – active listening, empathy, addressing team members' concerns, don't leave any issue unaddressed.

Let us move ahead and foster meaningful connections in life. Is it essential in your professional or personal life? I invite you to visit our college life.

We used to get group projects and have class discussions on different topics. Right? I can see the spark in your eyes. It is always wonderful to revisit our college days.

COLLEGE LIFE

Who were those students who were also getting attention and better academic results?

Students who communicated effectively and collaborated with their peers! You are right.

"By actively listening to each other's ideas, sharing diverse perspectives, and building rapport with fellow students, individuals can foster meaningful connections that enhance their learning experience and contribute to their overall success in college."

PERSONAL LIFE

What is the role of effective communication in personal life?

Effective communication is crucial in building trust, resolving conflicts, and maintaining emotional intimacy in personal relationships, such as friendships or romantic partnerships.

"Couples who openly communicate their feelings, listen empathetically to each other's concerns, and express appreciation for one another are more likely to form deeper and more fulfilling connections that withstand the test of time."

PROFESSIONAL LIFE

You can resonate easily if you look around you. If you have a colleague with solid communication skills, he effectively conveys his ideas, collaborates with colleagues, and builds relationships with clients quickly and faster. He is often recognized for his contributions by the seniors and gets career advancement faster.

"By fostering meaningful connections with co-workers, managers, and clients, individuals can create a supportive work environment, facilitate teamwork, and achieve their professional goals more effectively."

SOCIAL LIFE

Individuals who practice empathy, active listening, and genuine engagement are likelier to establish meaningful connections with family members, neighbors, or strangers.

"By demonstrating respect, understanding, and kindness in their interactions, people can forge strong bonds, cultivate a sense of community, and contribute positively to the well-being of those around them."

LONG-TERM SUCCESS

My experience suggests that leaders or business people who prioritize building meaningful connections with their team members, customers, and stakeholders are better positioned to achieve long-term success.

"By fostering a culture of open communication, trust, and collaboration, these individuals can inspire loyalty, drive innovation, and create sustainable relationships that fuel growth and prosperity."

These examples demonstrate how effective communication and meaningful connections are essential in all areas of life, from academic pursuits and personal relationships to professional endeavors and community engagement. By understanding the importance of fostering meaningful connections, you can cultivate richer, more meaningful experiences and achieve tremendous success in your personal and professional life.

STORYTIME

My grandfather was known for his generosity and compassion. In those days, the banking system could have been more robust, and villagers depended on moneylenders for every need, small or big. They were forced to pay heavy interest as there was no option other than these lenders. Once there was drought, and Ramdas's(To know more about Ramdas, Please read the previous episodes – The One Thing, How to Go Beyond Strength, Rising Together and Goal

Setting) grandfather had encountered financial hardships, struggling to repay a loan that burdened his family with heavy interest and principal payments.

My grandfather came forward to support and aid Ramdas's family during times of dire need. He paid all the dues on their behalf. This kindness alleviated their financial burdens and forged a deep and lasting bond between the two families.

Grateful for my grandfather's unwavering support and generosity, Ramdas's family remained fiercely loyal to my family, extending their heartfelt gratitude and loyalty through generations. Over the years, this meaningful connection transcended mere acquaintanceship, evolving into a cherished bond rooted in mutual respect, trust, and support.

Despite facing various challenges and adversities, the enduring friendship between my family and Ramdas's family is a source of strength and resilience. Both families found solace in each other's company through their unwavering loyalty and support. Sharing joys and sorrows, triumphs and tribulations.

This story showcases the emotional and psychological benefits of fostering meaningful connections.

1. Sense of belonging: Ramdas's family found a sense of belonging and security in their relationship with my family. They knew they had a reliable source of support and assistance in times of need.

2. Reduced loneliness: Both families experienced reduced loneliness and isolation through their bond. They found comfort and companionship in each other's presence.

3. Emotional support: My grandfather's selfless act of kindness gave Ramdas's family emotional stability and reassurance during their financial struggles. This fostered resilience and hope for a better future.

4. Mutual empathy and understanding: The connection between these two families was built on mutual empathy and understanding. They shared each other's joys and sorrows, strengthening their bond over time.

5. Increased life satisfaction: Their meaningful connection brought greater satisfaction and fulfillment to their lives. It enriched their experiences and strengthened their sense of community and belonging.

I hope you are getting the benefits of meaningful connections and will build better connections in your life. Is there another benefit of meaningful connections?

Yes, of course, there is. Let us discuss-

Developing meaningful connections with others is crucial in enhancing self-esteem and self-worth. When individuals cultivate deep and authentic relationships based on mutual respect, understanding, and support, they often experience a significant boost in their sense of value and self-assurance.

One fundamental way meaningful connections contribute to improved self-esteem is through validation and affirmation.

When we engage in meaningful interactions with others, we receive feedback and validation that reinforce our sense of worth and competence. Positive affirmations, expressions of appreciation, and acts of kindness from those we care about can profoundly impact our self-perception, helping us recognize our strengths, capabilities, and inherent worth.

Not only this, but furthermore, meaningful connections provide a supportive framework for personal growth and development. When we surround ourselves with people who believe in us, encourage our aspirations, and challenge us to reach our full potential, we are likelier to believe in ourselves and pursue our goals with confidence and determination. The encouragement and support from meaningful relationships buffer against self-doubt and insecurity, empowering us to overcome obstacles and pursue our dreams with resilience and tenacity.

Sense of belonging and acceptance are fundamental psychological needs. When we feel accepted and valued by others, we are more likely to accept and value ourselves. Knowing that we have a supportive network of friends, family, and colleagues who accept us for who we are, our flaws and all, allows us to embrace our authentic selves and celebrate our unique qualities without fear of judgment or rejection.

Moreover, meaningful connections provide a source of emotional stability and security. During times of adversity or uncertainty, knowing that we have trusted allies who have our backs can provide a sense of reassurance and comfort. This emotional support makes us more confident about facing challenges and overcoming obstacles.

In summary:

Cultivating deep and authentic relationships based on mutual respect, understanding, and support can lead to a profound sense of validation, belonging, and acceptance. These meaningful connections catalyze personal growth, providing the encouragement, support, and emotional stability needed to overcome obstacles and thrive in all aspects of life.

COMMUNICATION BARRIERS

There are many factors responsible for hindering the effectiveness of interpersonal interactions. Some common communication barriers are as follows;

1. **Lack of Clarity:** Language barriers, complex jargon, and vague expressions can obscure the intended meaning of communication.

For example, some people use specialized language that may be difficult for individuals without specific expertise or knowledge to understand –"The project requires the implementation of a comprehensive CRM system with integrated API functionality to optimize data analytics and facilitate seamless cross-platform integration."

Vague expressions involve ambiguous or imprecise language that needs more clarity. For example, "We need to improve customer satisfaction levels and enhance user experience to drive better results."

As a leader, you should refrain from language hindering effective communication and confusing your team members.

The Leader, a speaker in this case, should have an objective to simplify the message by removing technical terms and focusing on the main objective: " Enhance customer relationship through system upgrade."

We need to upgrade our customer management system to understand our customers better and improve how we interact with them across different platforms.

Similarly, this leader could have simplified his message by saying, "We aim to make our customers happier and ensure they have a smoother experience when using our services, leading to improved performance and outcomes."

Remember- "It's important to strive for clarity and simplicity in communication to ensure messages are understood accurately by all team members."

2. **Poor Listening Skills-** Ineffective listening, such as selective hearing or distracted listening, prevents individuals from fully understanding and empathizing with others' perspectives.

3. **Cultural Difference-** Differences in nonverbal cues, such as body language and gestures, may be misinterpreted across cultures. Variations in cultural norms, values, and communication styles can create misunderstandings and breakdowns. For example, in some cultures, people don't confront others directly and don't show their disagreement in an open forum as they consider it rude. Risk- Important decisions may be made with consideration of the full range of viewpoints, hindering collaboration and innovation within multicultural teams.

4. **Emotional Barriers—Many leaders show strong emotions, which may lead to defensive responses. For example**, Anger, fear, or anxiety are strong

emotions that can disrupt communication by clouding judgment and inhibiting rational thinking.

5. Perceptual Differences- Past experiences, contrasting viewpoints, beliefs, and biases can create communication barriers.

6. Physical Barriers- or environmental factors, such as noise, distractions, or distance- can impede communication, making it difficult to hear, concentrate, or maintain visual contact. Remember- "This may occur in both face-to-face and virtual communication settings."

7. Hierarchical Barriers- in some organizations or societies, power differentials and hierarchical structure create a barrier to open communication. In such an atmosphere, people feel uncomfortable and hesitate to voice their opinions or concerns. This may lead to a need for more transparency and trust. And

8. Technical Barriers—Nowadays, technology is used as a communication tool. Technical glitches, connectivity issues, or even familiarity with communication technologies may pose challenges.

My suggestion: Please identify and address these communication barriers to enhance your communication skills., foster meaningful connections, and overcome obstacles to effective interpersonal interactions.

EXERCISE

Can you list out some more barriers to effective communication?

Case study: You are a team leader and lead a diverse team of professionals from different cultural backgrounds. During a team meeting, you propose a new strategy for improving market share for your Organization in the next 12 months. However, one team member from a culture that values hierarchy and authority appears hesitant to express his opinion or offer.

You gave feedback openly in front of the group. As a result, you noticed a need for more participation from this team member, which may impact the plan's success.

QUESTIONS

1. What potential barriers to effective communication may arise due to cultural differences?
2. How can you adapt your communication approach to ensure all team members feel comfortable expressing their perspectives and contributing to the discussion?

MY MESSAGE TO BUILDING RAPPORT

Building rapport is essential for fostering meaningful connections in personal and professional life. To establish rapport, one should start by showing genuine interest in others and actively listening to their perspectives and experiences.

Engage in open and authentic communication, demonstrating empathy and understanding.

Find common ground and shared interest to create a sense of connection and mutual trust.

Be respectful, reliable, and consistent in your interactions, demonstrating your commitment to building a solid relationship.

As you read the "Mastering the Art of Communication" pages, you've gained invaluable insights and practical strategies to enhance your interpersonal skills and cultivate meaningful connections. It's time to put your newfound knowledge into action and embark on a personal and professional growth journey. At the same time, assertive communication is essential. It is vital to understand assertiveness in communication and why it is crucial.

THE POWER OF ASSERTIVE COMMUNICATION

"Assertiveness is not what you do, and it's who you are."

- Shakti Gawain

In mastering communication, one of the essential skills to cultivate is assertiveness. Why assertive communication?

Assertive communication allows you to express your thoughts, feelings and needs confidently and respectfully. It is equally important to respect the feelings and opinions of others. We will learn and explore practical strategies to harness its potential in various aspects of life.

We will uncover the fundamental principles of assertiveness and learn how this can empower us to navigate challenging situations with grace and confidence.

In the broad picture of communication, three distinct colors emerge: passive acquiescence, aggressive confrontation, and assertive expression.

PASSIVE COMMUNICATION

Passive communication often manifests as silence, compliance, or avoidance of conflict, sacrificing one's needs and desires to comfort or please others.

On the other end of the spectrum lies aggressive communication, characterized by dominance, hostility, and a disregard for the feelings and opinions of others.

ASSERTIVE COMMUNICATION

Assertive communication embodies a delicate balance—a middle ground where you confidently and respectfully express your thoughts, feelings, and needs while also honoring the perspectives of others. Benefits of being assertive: Assertiveness allows you to set clear boundaries, assert your values, and advocate for yourself without resorting to manipulation or aggression. Embracing assertive communication can positively impact every aspect of life. It promotes genuine connections based on trust, mutual respect, and honest communication. In situations where conflicts arise, assertiveness helps you resolve them constructively and with empathy.

Additionally, assertive communication can boost your self-confidence and enable you to assert your worth confidently in pursuing your goals.

Let's explore the importance of assertive communication and its transformational power in our personal and professional lives.

STORYTIME

Sweta works in an office with tight deadlines and high tensions in one of her companies. Despite being a dedicated employee, she is overwhelmed with mounting tasks and conflicting priorities. Sweta needs help to voice her concerns and advocate for her needs in team meetings. She fears backlash or rejection from her colleagues and silently shoulders the burden.

One day, during a particularly hectic week of preparations for next year's budget meetings, Sweta reaches her breaking point. Feeling undervalued and unheard, she confides in her manager, John. With trepidation, she schedules a meeting to discuss her workload and seek support. As Sweta nervously articulates her concerns, John listens attentively. His expression reflects genuine empathy and understanding. Rather than dismissing her fears or assigning blame, he acknowledges the validity of her feelings and offers practical solutions to alleviate her stress.

This open and honest exchange marks a profound shift for Sweta. She learns the importance of assertive communication, i.e., expressing herself confidently and respectfully even in challenging situations. Inspired by John's example, Sweta begins to assert her boundaries, communicate her needs, and advocate for herself with newfound courage and conviction.

LESSONS LEARNED

1. The Power of Open Communication: Open and honest communication is vital in fostering understanding and resolving conflict. As you notice, by voicing her concerns to her manager, Sweta initiates a dialogue that leads to positive change.

2. Impact of Active Listening: John's attentive listening and empathetic response demonstrate the transformative power of active listening. His ability to validate Sweta's feelings and offer meaningful support creates a supportive environment for her to express herself.

3. The Value of Assertive Communication: Sweta's journey underscores the significance of assertive communication in advocating for one's needs and asserting boundaries. BY speaking up assertively, she asserts her worth and initiates positive change in her work environment.

4. Building Trust and Respect: through their open dialogue and mutual respect, Sweta and John strengthen their professional relationship and build trust. This foundation of trust enables them to collaborate effectively and address challenges together.

The story of Sweta emphasizes the importance of communication, active listening, assertiveness, and building trust in fostering positive relationships and achieving mutual understanding and support in both personal and professional life.

PRINCIPLES OF ASSERTIVE COMMUNICATION

Assertive communication is guided by several fundamental principles that empower you to express yourself confidently, respectfully, and effectively. I am sharing a few principles of assertive communication:

1- Respect for the individual: It involves expressing thoughts, feelings, and needs with self-respect while also respecting the perspectives and boundaries of others.

2- Clear and Direct Expression: Assertive communication is characterized by transparency. Direct and specific expression. It involves stating opinions, making requests, and setting boundaries without ambiguity or passive-aggressive behavior.

3- Active Listening: Assertive communicators actively listen to others, seeking to understand their perspectives and feelings without judgment or interruption. They always validate other people's experiences and demonstrate empathy and understanding.

4- Non-Verbal Assertiveness: Non-verbal cues, such as eye contact, body language, and tone of voice, play a crucial role in assertive communication. Maintain a confident posture, make appropriate eye contact, and use a calm and assertive tone.

5- Conflict Resolution: Assertive communication facilitates constructive resolution by encouraging open dialogue, active listening, and collaborative problem-solving. This helps you to address conflicts directly, express concerns, and seek mutually beneficial solutions.

6- **Self-awareness:** You must be self-aware and manage your emotions effectively. Express yourself assertively without becoming defensive or aggressive.

My suggestion: *"Practice these Principles and cultivate communication skills that promote mutual respect, understanding, and positive relationships in various personal and professional contexts."*

Practice makes things permanent. I suggest some practices and techniques of assertive communication:

1. Remember to use "I" statements to express your feelings, thoughts, and needs directly and assertively. This can make a significant difference in communication. For example, saying, "You never listen to me," is not an example of assertive communication. Instead, try using an "I" statement like "I feel frustrated when I don't feel heard" to express yourself assertively.

2. Active Listening: Make eye contact by giving full attention to the speaker. Nodding and paraphrasing will ensure understanding. This will encourage open dialogue.

3. Fogging: let me share about Fogging first. Fogging is a technique used in assertive communication to respond calmly and effectively to criticism, disagreement, or negative feedback. The goal of fogging is to acknowledge the validity of the other person's perspective without becoming defensive or argumentative.

This can defuse tension and maintain open communication while asserting your viewpoint or boundaries.

Let me share one example-

If I criticize you by saying, "You're always so disorganized," You can use fogging to respond assertively without becoming defensive. You might say, "I can understand why you see it that way. I've had some organizational challenges lately, but I'm improving my systems."

Use fogging to respond calmly to criticism or disagreement without becoming defensive. Acknowledge the validity of the other person's perspective while maintaining your position. For example- "I can see why you might feel that way, but I have a different viewpoint."

4. Assertive Repetition: use this technique to restate your position assertively. In your leadership journey, you may come across situations when you are facing resistance or even refusal of your proposals. This technique becomes very useful in managing those situations. Use this technique- "Repeat your message calmly and firmly, without becoming argumentative or aggressive."

5. Assertive Body Language: Stand upright while addressing your team. Sit upright, make eye contact, and maintain an open posture during the decision. Avoid crossing your arms, as this signals defensiveness. Other defensive gestures are covering the throat or abdomen, pointing fingers, and wagging a finger.

You can identify quickly if the speaker is defensive in his approach:

If he is avoiding eye contact.

If he interrupts others

If he speaks loudly or uses sarcasm.

If he leans back in his chair, etc.

6. Saying No: learn the art of saying 'No' assertively when you need to say 'NO' to decline a request. You might have experienced some people wanting to say no but not being able to communicate clearly and sounding like 'Yes.'

Technique to say No- be direct but respectful, and briefly explain if necessary. For example, "I appreciate the offer, but I cannot commit to that right now."

7. Assertive Problem-Solving: approach conflicts or disagreements assertively by focusing on finding mutually beneficial solutions.

Technique:

Use collaborative problem-solving techniques, such as brainstorming or the why-why technique. Brainstorming helps generate new ideas, and the why-why technique helps you find the root cause of the problem.

Let me share a scenario with you. It was around 2002, and my team was experiencing a decline in productivity. Members needed help meeting project deadlines.

Let me take you directly to the meeting room. It was team leader, so read 'Team Leader' when I say Me.

Me- Why do you think we're experiencing a decline in productivity?

Team Member: Because we need more tasks.

Me: Why do you feel overwhelmed?

Team Member: Because we need to prioritize tasks more effectively.

Me: Why do you think we need to prioritize tasks more effectively?

Team Member: We still need to establish clear project goals and priorities.

Me: Why have we yet to establish clear project goals and priorities?

Team Member: Because we still need to have a thorough discussion about project objectives and deadlines.

As you can see from my experience, the team uncovered the root cause of the productivity decline as "a lack of project goals and priorities."

Remember: "Brainstorming and the why-why technique serve different purposes and can be used complementarily in problem-solving and decision-making processes."

Brainstorming: Use to generate ideas or solutions.

The Why-Why: Use to uncover underlying reasons or causes.

EXERCISE

One of your team members says, Sir, I want to quit my Job."- using the "why-why" technique, explore their reasons further:

Write your top 3 lessons that you have learned from these chapters.

1.

2.

3.

Where to use the Why-Why technique and

When to use brainstorming?

It is time to take action...

CALL FOR ACTION

Here are some actionable steps to continue honing your communication skills and reaping the benefits of effective communication in your daily life.

1. Practice Active Listening: Commit to becoming a more attentive and empathetic listener in your interactions with others. Take the time to truly understand their perspectives and experiences, and resist the urge to interrupt or pass judgment.

2. Cultivate Empathy and Understanding: Make a conscious effort to put yourself in other's shoes and empathize with their thoughts, feelings, and needs. Approach every interaction with an open heart and a willingness to connect on a deeper level.

3. Communicate with Clarity and Precision: Strive to articulate your thoughts and ideas clearly and precisely, using language easily understood by others. Avoid ambiguity and confusion by being direct and concise in your communication.

4. Foster Meaningful Connections: invest time and effort in building genuine relationships with those around you. Show appreciation for their unique qualities and perspectives and respect and kindness in your interactions.

5. Embrace Diversity and Inclusion: celebrate the richness of cultural diversity and embrace the opportunity to learn from others' backgrounds and experiences. Be open-

minded and curious about different perspectives, and challenge yourself to step outside your comfort zone.

6. Seek Feedback and Continuous Improvement: solicit feedback from trusted friends, colleagues, or mentors on your communication style and areas of growth. Embrace constructive criticism as an opportunity for learning and improvement.

7. Set Communication Goals: identify specific communication goals that align with your personal and professional aspirations. Whether becoming a more confident public speaker, resolving conflicts more effectively, or building stronger relationships, set actionable goals and track your progress over time.

I can assure you by committing to these actionable steps, you'll not only enhance your communication skills but also contribute to a more harmonious and connected world,

Remember: effective communication is not just a skill—it's a lifelong journey of growth, learning, and connection. Let "Mastering the Art of Communication" be your guide as you continue on this transformative path.

It is time now to summarize what we have learned.

SUMMARY AND TAKE-HOME MESSAGE

"Mastering the Art of Communication" is a guide that will help you to improve your interpersonal skills, create meaningful connections, and handle communication challenges with confidence and clarity. In these chapters, you have seen the blend of practical strategies, real-life examples, and insightful wisdom, which will help you quickly navigate communication. For your reference and take-home message, here is a chapter-wise summary -

CHAPTER 1

Effective communication is the art of conveying messages accurately and persuasively while listening actively and empathetically to others—the key elements of effective communication.

Master the Key Elements that we learned in this chapter, which are as follows-

Clarity, Active Listening, Empathy, feedback, awareness of nonverbal cues, adaptability, respect, purposefulness, conflict resolution, and commitment to improvement.

These elements will help you articulate your thoughts and ideas. Improving your listening will help you better understand your team members. Listening to your team members' voices will make them feel valued, which will help you foster meaningful connections.

Characteristics of meaningful connections are-

Authenticity- Genuine expression of thought, feelings, and experiences with fear of judgment.

Empathy- Understanding and sharing the feelings of others.

Trust- Confidence in the reliability and integrity of the other person.

Respect- Acknowledgment of each other's individuality.

Communication- open and honest dialogue that facilitates deep understanding and connection.

Shared values and interests- Alignments in beliefs, goals, and interests, creating common ground for connection.

Emotional support- Providing comfort, encouragement, and assistance during times of need.

Constructive feedback and encouragement will help your team members grow and develop.

CHAPTER 2

In this chapter, we have discussed the principles of effective communication. Let us revisit these principles-

Clarity—ensure your message is clear, concise, and easily understood by your team members. We have learned to avoid jargon.

Empathy- empathize with the thoughts, feelings, and perspectives of others.

Active listening- practice reflective listening techniques, such as paraphrasing and summarizing.

Respect- treat everyone with respect and dignity. Avoid disrespectful behavior.

Authenticity- communicate with sincerity, honesty, and authenticity. Be genuine in expressing yourself.

Adaptability- be flexible and adaptive in your communication approach to accommodate different situations.

Feedback- seek and provide constructive feedback to enhance communication effectiveness. Encourage open dialogue. Ask for clarification when needed, and be receptive to feedback from others.

Nonverbal Communication- pay attention to nonverbal cues such as body language, facial expression, and tone of voice.

Confidence- communicate with confidence and assertiveness. Coney your message with clarity and conviction. Project confidence through your posture and tone of voice.

Practice these principles to enhance your communication effectiveness and to foster meaningful connections.

CHAPTER 3

Listening is a sign of respect.

Active listening is a fundamental component of effective communication, and we all know this; still, you find people around you who believe in telling and not in listening. Effective communication involves expressing ourselves clearly and actively listening to others.

We have explored the dynamic interplay between telling and articulating our thoughts and ideas.

And listening- attentively engaging with the perspectives and emotions of others.

We learned how to craft compelling narratives. Through practical exercises and real-life examples, we hone our storytelling skills and discover the power of narrative in shaping perceptions and influencing outcomes.

Turning our attention to the skill of listening, we explored the art of attentive and empathetic engagement. Active listening, characterized by presence, empathy, and nonverbal cues, forms the foundation of meaningful communication. We also explored the role of feedback, clarification, and validation in fostering mutual understanding and collaboration.

CHAPTER 4

We have understood the concept of empathy as the ability to understand and share the feelings of others.

We explored the importance of empathy in effective communication and building meaningful connections.

We have recognized the role of empathy in fostering trust, rapport, and mutual respect in interpersonal relationships.

We learned how active listening can cultivate empathy and discussed its role in conflict resolution, collaboration, and teamwork.

CHAPTER 5

In this chapter, we have understood the principles of persuasion as the art of influencing others' beliefs, attitudes, and behaviors.

We explored the psychology behind persuasion, including ethical and practical techniques in various contexts, such as marketing, sales, and negotiation.

Another discussion was on the role of storytelling, social proof, and emotional appeals in persuasive messaging.

We learned about Dr.Cialdini's six principles of persuasion, which are as follows.

1- Reciprocity

2- Commitment and Consistency

3- Social Proof

4- Authority

5- Liking

6- Scarcity

CHAPTER 6

In this chapter, we have recognized the importance of building genuine connections with others based on trust, respect, and empathy.

We have explored the benefits of meaningful connections in fostering collaboration, teamwork, and mutual support.

Our other learning was establishing rapport and cultivating authentic relationships through active listening, empathy, and open communication.

Our action point from this chapter was to recognize the role of cultural diversity and inclusivity in fostering meaningful connections across different backgrounds and perspectives.

We have learned the barriers to communication and how to overcome these barriers.

I have requested that you apply what you have learned daily and in relationships. Whether communicating with colleagues in the workplace, navigating family dynamics at home, or engaging with strangers in the community, readers discover how to harness the power of effective communication to achieve our goals and foster positive outcomes.

Power of Assertive Communication

Assertive communication allows you to express your thoughts, feelings and needs confidently and respectfully.

It is equally important to respect the feelings and opinions of others.

We learned to explore practical strategies to harness its potential in various aspects of life.

Another critical lesson was how assertive communication empowers you to navigate challenging situations gracefully and confidently.

We have learned three distinct colors of assertive communication-

passive acquiescence, aggressive confrontation, and assertive expression.

FINAL CHAPTER- CALL FOR ACTION

"Communication is the fuel that ignites the flames of understanding, connection, and change."

- Unknown

Practice Action Listening

Cultivate empathy and understanding

Communicate with clarity and precision

Foster Meaningful connections

Embrace Diversity and Inclusion

Seek feedback and continuous improvement

Set Communication Goals.

Please make a list of action points that you would like to practice to be a good communicator in your life, be it personal life or professional life.

1.

2.

3.

4.

5.

FINAL STORY

In my village, there was an extraordinary elderly couple that we used to call Dada and Dadi or Grandfather and Grandmother. They were known for their unwavering bond and deep love for one another. Despite the passage of time, they remained inseparable, their hearts entwined in a timeless dance of companionship and understanding.

One day, my friends and I gathered the courage to ask our grandparents (Dada and Dadi) about the secret to their enduring relationship. We were captivated by the warmth and love that radiated from them. With a gentle smile and eyes twinkling with wisdom, grandfather took the grandmother's hand and shared their timeless wisdom. He said, "My dear boys, it's all about communication. We've shared our hopes, dreams, and fears for decades, never hesitating to speak our truth and listen with an open heart."

As young boys, we were curious about their fears and dreams. Grandmother spoke first, her voice soft yet filled with depth. "Our fear of loneliness and our dream to see our grandchildren growing and playing with us," She shared. Grandfather nodded in agreement, adding, "Communication goes beyond mere words, my dear children. It's about the silent moments of understanding, the tender gestures of affection, and the unwavering support we offer each other every step of the way."

They held hands tightly with emotion, and the warmth in my heart lingers. They left for heaven years ago, but their blessings and wisdom guide us.

Thank you for being with me on this Journey of effective communication.

With warm Regards

ABOUT THE AUTHOR

 JP Pathak emerges as a seasoned professional in sales, management, training, and coaching, with a remarkable journey spanning over 35 years. As a dedicated student of sales and management, he has honed his expertise as a practitioner and mentor, guiding individuals to discover their "One Thing" that propels them toward realizing their dreams and purpose.

Throughout his extensive career, JP has navigated the intricacies of sales and marketing, earning a reputation as a sales superstar.

One of JP's distinctive qualities lies in his ability to simplify complex concepts, making them accessible and understandable for his audience. His training and coaching methods are infused with humor, creating an environment that fosters relaxation and comfort, even in challenging situations or when dealing with difficult-to-manage individuals.

JP's effectiveness as a trainer is not solely based on his vast experience but is enriched by his capacity to weave anecdotes and small stories into his teachings. These narratives serve as memorable lessons, ensuring that the knowledge imparted remains ingrained in the minds of his students for an extended period.

JP imparts wisdom and creates an engaging and enjoyable learning experience by incorporating humor and storytelling.

Beyond his professional endeavors, JP Pathak is a science graduate who shares his life with his wife and two daughters. His commitment extends beyond individual growth, as he actively contributes to developing people and organizations. Through his training and coaching initiatives, JP leaves an indelible mark on the journey of those he guides, fostering growth and success.

OTHER BOOKS WRITTEN BY THE AUTHOR

Click this book

Click this book

Click this book

Click this book

DISCLAIMER

This book is for informational purposes only. Readers acknowledge that the author does not render legal, financial, medical, or professional advice. The content within this book has been derived from various sources. Please consult a licensed professional before attempting any techniques outlined in this book.

By reading this document, the reader agrees that under no circumstances is the author responsible for any direct or indirect losses incurred due to the use of the information contained within this document, including but not limited to errors, omissions, or inaccuracies. Adherence to all applicable laws and regulations, including international, federal, state, and local governing professional licensing, business practices, advertising, and all other jurisdictions, is the sole responsibility of the purchaser or reader. Neither the author nor the publisher assumes any responsibility or liability on behalf of the purchaser or reader of these materials. Any perceived slight of any individual or organization is purely unintentional.

MAY I ASK YOU A FAVOR?

First, I want to say a big thanks for reading this book. You could have chosen any other book, but you took mine, and I appreciate this. I hope you have a few actionable insights that can positively impact your daily life.

Can I ask for 30 seconds more of your time?

I'd love it if you could leave a review of the book. That will help me grow my readership by encouraging folks to take a chance on my books.

Keeping it straight - *reviews are the lifeblood of any author.*

It will take less than a minute of your time but will tremendously help me reach out to more people. **Kindly provide your review at the store you bought this book from.** And I'd love to see your review. Thanks for your support.

www.ingramcontent.com/pod-product-compliance
Lightning Source LLC
Chambersburg PA
CBHW070157230526
45471CB00002B/702